# Spilling the Beans on...

# COMPUTERS

First published in 2001 by Miles Kelly Publishing,
Bardfield Centre, Great Bardfield, Essex CM7 4SL
Info@mileskelly.net

Printed in Italy

ISBN 1-84236-011-6

24681097531

Visit us on the web:
www.mileskelly.net

Cover design and illustration: Inc
Layout design: Mackerel

# Spilling the Beans on...
# COMPUTERS

## by Edmond Hugo
### Edited by Vic Parker

Illustrations   Martin Remphry

Miles Kelly
PUBLISHING

# CONTENTS

# WHO WANTS TO BE A MILLIONAIRE?

*Hands up – who wants to be Bill Gates?*

*Who's Bill Gates?*

What do you mean, who's Bill Gates? I reply in astonishment. He's only the richest man on Planet Earth, that's who. And I don't mean possibly the richest man on Planet Earth, I mean definitely, absolutely, everybody-who-is-anybody-agrees-that-he-really-really-is the richest man on Planet Earth.

Just imagine it for a second. Not just richer than the exceedingly rich David Beckham and Posh Spice, but richer than the entire Manchester United football team and all the Spice Girls put together. Richer than tycoon Richard Branson, who owns airlines, railway companies, fizzy drinks firms and record labels. Richer than the Queen, with all her jewels, castles and palaces. Richer than the Sultan of Brunei, who is so ridiculously rich he can afford to hire multi-millionaire Michael Jackson to perform at a private party for his friends!

Now hands up, who wants to be Bill Gates? (Yes, me too, actually . . . )

Bill Gates. It's a pretty ordinary name, isn't it? You might expect the richest person on Planet Earth to be called something much more impressive, like perhaps Sir Cosmo Lush or maybe Princess Esmeralda Divine. So how come this normal-sounding man – a plain 'Mister' – has ended up having so much cash that he can buy absolutely anything. Just think of it, anything – that he wants.

Computers, that's how.

Bill Gates is the founder and owner of Microsoft, the largest computer software company in the world. Almost every computer in every home, office, shop, train/bus/police station, theme park, leisure centre, theatre, hospital, library etc. in the entire world uses Microsoft software of some sort or another. That's an awful lot of software, an awful lot of money for Microsoft, and an awful lot of money in the Bill Gates' bank account.

And wait for this . . . many people would say that not only is Bill Gates the richest man in the world, he is also the luckiest man in the world. Because, of course, Microsoft doesn't just make office software such as word processing, and graphic design and spreadsheet packages –

Microsoft also makes computer games. Yes, Bill Gates is the owner of the biggest, best, most exciting computer gaming company on the globe. It would be true to say that he is the Willy Wonka of the computer world.

*Thanks! So now you've made me green with envy! But why are you telling me all this? What's in it for me?*

Well – hark, I bring thee glad tidings. If sitting at a computer is your idea of heaven, you too can become seriously wealthy by doing it for a living. And what could be better than spending all day doing the thing you most enjoy and getting paid pots of cash for it? Yes, just like our friend Bill, you can make it big in computers. And this humble little book will tell you all you need to know.

*Great! Let's get on with it then.*

Steady on, there's no need to rush, is there? First, before we look at the glorious future that lies ahead of you, I want to take you back . . . back . . . back . . . back to the nightmare that was life BC – life Before Computers.

Imagine you are a medieval peasant and the Lord of the Manor has put you to work in his storehouse as his Official Bean Counter. Every day, you sit at the foot of his Lordship's mountain of dried beans and count them – one by one. But it's not as easy as it sounds. For a start off, it's mind-numbingly boring. So boring that you often lose concentration – then you have to go right back to the beginning and start again. And what about when you have to nip to the loo? It's almost impossible to keep track of where you are and you nearly always make a mistake. As you can imagine, the Lord of the Manor is not pleased when his Official Bean Counter gets it wrong – not pleased at all. You've spent more hours hung upside down by your toes than you care to remember. How you wish there was a machine that could do the counting for you . . .

**1642**   Teenage French whizkid Blaise Pascal invents a machine that can add up huge columns of figures, to help his father in his job as Chief Tax Collector for Rouen. The world's first calculator is born (shame it's far too late for all medieval Official Bean Counters) . . .

**nearly 200 years ago**

Englishman Charles Babbage, a Professor of Maths, designs the first real computer. Called 'The Difference Engine', it looks like the inside of an enormous clock, with gears and turning wheels to do the work, and numbered dials to display the answers (electricity isn't understood until the early 1800s). It is supposed to be able to do complicated sums with 100% accuracy – but no one ever finds out whether it really can, as Babbage never actually builds it.

## 1930s and 1940s

The first electrical and electronic computers are built in Britain and America. They are enormous, because of the size of the components. One of the first is called ENIAC (Electronic Numerical Integrator and Computer) and weighs 30 tonnes. It can't store data or programs, so every time someone wants to run a new program, it has to be completely rewired!

**1950s** Computers get smaller, faster and smarter, but they're still huge and very slow and hard to use. There are no CDs yet, so programs have to be loaded on punched cards or paper-tape, and data is stored on huge spools of magnetic tape – like an audio cassette, but 10 or 15 times bigger. Only the biggest, richest companies can afford the price or space to have a computer. No one dreams there will one day be computers for use in the home.

**1959** An American firm called Texas Instruments discovers that tiny circuits can be printed onto a minute piece of silicon in the same way that a photograph can be printed onto paper. Companies begin to experiment with making smaller and smaller circuits . . . .

**1971** A company called Intel manage to get all their components for a computer onto just one piece of silicon. They describe it as a computer on a chip – or a microchip. Now the modern, personal computer is possible . . .

*Phew!* Who wants to be a medieval Official Bean Counter, after all?

# GET WITH THE PROGRAM

Computers are so fast and so apparently clever, that it's sometimes hard to remember that they are only tools. Computers are only as good as the programs that people write for them, and how other people use those applications. Or, to put it more simply: garbage in, garbage out.

And when I say computers, I don't just mean the big beige things that sit on people's desks. Some of the most advanced computers today – the really really smart ones – are tiny microchips. You'd have to have been living in a cupboard for the past ten years not to notice how these things have completely changed our lives. Now you can:

↗ organise your life with a hand-held computer the size of a bar of soap, which

will function as your
diary, address book,
wordprocessor,
calculator,
measurement-
converter, map-
finder, appointment
reminder . . . just
about the only
thing these devices
don't do is get
you dressed in the
morning!

➤ buy cars that will warn you if there's a
problem with the engine and tell you what
the temperature is outside, that will work
out the best road route for you and display
it on a dashboard screen, and that will lock
themselves if you forget to.

➤ own a mobile phone that doesn't need wires
to link up to the Internet or send emails.

The list goes on and on. And don't forget –
behind all of these really, really clever

computer devices are really, really
clever people. The people who make it big
in computers are clever in not just one, but
two ways:

1 As you might expect, they're clever at
computer science and new innovations and
inventions in IT.

2 But they're also clever at the old-fashioned
skills necessary for success in any business,
such as:

- the ability and willingness to learn new
things
- good communications skills in speaking
and writing
- good numeracy skills
- the ability to work well on your own and
in a team
- the ability to think for yourself and make
decisions
- creativity – especially in solving
problems.

So let's start by tackling the first part: making
sure you're clued-up about the essential
technology. After all, have you ever stopped to
wonder what is actually going on inside your PC?

# PC-POWER

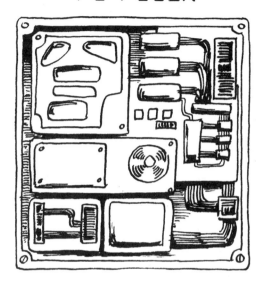

It looks a bit like a model town, doesn't it? The dark rectangular bits could be houses and the shiny lines running between them could be paths or roads or railway lines or telephone wires.

The people who live in this town are not normal people. They're superheroes. And as is usual for superheroes, they each have a special power. But there is a snag. Their special power is all they can do – just that one thing. They're completely useless at anything else.

Meet the superhero boss – the Processor (or Pentium, to his friends). He's a fantastic organizer and mathematician. He can do sums amazingly fast and he has the special power of knowing exactly who to call to get anything done. He is so good at organizing that he has been given the job of running the whole town. The only problem is that he can't remember anything. Nothing. Not a sausage. Every time the computer is switched on he wakes up and finds he has forgotten all about everything he organized the day before. He can't remember the simplest task!

Luckily, living close by is RAM, a superhero with amazing memory powers. RAM can remember anything in perfect detail. And any information that she can't be bothered to memorize she stores in an extension she's had built onto her house – a room in the shape of a big hard disk.

The most important thing that RAM remembers are all the laws of the town – everything that needs to be done to keep the water running, the streets clean and all the superheroes happy.

These laws are known as the Operating System.

However, RAM doesn't know how to use all the things she knows. She's like a chef who has memorized every recipe for every dish in the world, but doesn't know how to switch on a cooker, hasn't got the first idea how to chop up an onion, doesn't even know which way up a saucepan goes. She's got a fantastic memory, but on her own she's totally useless.

Further down the road live two more superheroes. Graphics Card can draw amazing pictures, but only if there's someone telling him exactly  where to put this line, or that dot, or what colour the grass and sky should be. His friend, Sound Card, can make wonderful music, but only

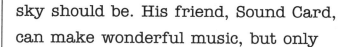 if every single note is written down and put in front of her. In fact, until she's been given the music, she can't make a sound of any sort – not a squeak, not a whisper.

On their own, each superhero is useless. But if they work together, using their special powers to help each other, they can do mind-boggling things.

However, unlike normal people, these superheroes don't go out to work. They stay in. You could say that they're super couch potatoes. They never leave their houses to go and meet each other, but just send each other messages instead. In fact, all around the town are special buses that can deliver messages from one superhero to the other.

One more thing. The superheroes don't use writing for their messages, they use a special number code. Another word for something in numbers is digital. That's why computer information is known as digital information.

OK, so now if you ever bump into Bill Gates at a cocktail party and want to beg for a job in his company, you can be confident that you can explain to him how a PC works. But are you going to be able to wow him with the other type of computer cleverness – good old-fashioned business skills? Try this little quiz to find out if you've got what it takes . . .

## BUSINESS-BRAIN OR BANANA-BRAIN?

### Questions

1 Your teacher has told you to give a
10-minute talk to the rest of your
class on the joys of keeping pet
guinea-pigs. How do you get on?

> **A** You sellotape your legs together
> to stop your knees from
> knocking, fumble for a
> handkerchief to wipe the
> feverish sweat from your brow,
> gulp down a glass of water in an
> effort to lubricate your Sahara-
> dry throat, and squeak: 'Um . . .
> Er . . . Well . . . Yes . . . Pinea-
> gigs - I mean, guinea-pigs . . .' (At
> this point the class dissolves into
> hysterical giggles.)

> **B** Say, 'Well, I have to say that I
> think keeping guinea-pigs is
> more boring than watching TV
> with the set turned off, and I

couldn't be bothered to find out anything about them – the end.'

**C** Explain, 'I don't actually keep guinea-pigs myself, but I spent last week at the library finding out all about them and also talking to friends who keep them as pets. I was amazed and fascinated to find out . . . ' (You go on to give a captivating 10-minute talk.)

**2** Your teacher asks you: 'If Tariq gets £14 pocket money per month and the new Blood, Guts and Gore computer game costs £35, how long will it take him to save up enough money to buy it – in days?'

Which of the following is more likely to happen:

**A** You pronounce the correct answer without a moment's hesitation.

**B** You get the answer right at the third attempt, with a little bit of help from your teacher.

**C** You give your calculator a bashing for half an hour and chew your pencil to shreds, then admit you haven't a clue.

**3** Your PE teacher tells you to work either on your own or in a pair to come up with a dance on the theme of 'Tragedy'. You'd quite like to work on your own, but your friend begs you to pair up with her.

**Do you:**

**A** Sit down and sulk. You hate dance anyway.

**B** Say 'no way' to your friend.

You perform the Steps routine you practised last week in front of your bedroom mirror (which your friend doesn't know) and you are the best in the class.

**C** Agree to work with your friend. You teach her a bit of your Steps routine, she teaches you some of her own ideas and together you're the best in the class.

**4** You're getting ready for a big night out, and you simply can't decide what to wear. Should it be the orange shirt with the brown swirls or the zebra-patterned mohair pullover? Then again, maybe you should just plump for your faithful old black pullover – even if it does have a hole under the arm. How do you decide?

**Do you:**

**A** Phone a mate whose opinion you trust – and then go with whatever they advise.

**B** Phone several mates, who all advise you differently – so you end up even more confused than before.

**C** Phone a mate whose opinion you trust – and then make up your own mind, taking their advice into consideration.

**5** Your teacher tells you to imagine that you are stranded on a desert island with only a penknife, a length of string, a blanket and a nearby palm tree for company. How do you cope?

**A** You sit on the sand and start crying.

**B** You use your penknife and the string to cut and sew the blanket into a jumper and trousers that wouldn't be out of place on the Paris catwalks. Then you shimmy up the palm tree, collect some coconuts, bash them open and sit down to a tasty feast. You're too busy enjoying yourself to start thinking of escape just yet . . .

**C** You use your penknife to saw the palm tree down and slice it into sticks. You make a warm, cosy, tent-style shelter from most of the blanket, the string and some of the sticks. You then make a big flag from another stick and the rest of the blanket, and build the remaining sticks into a massive signal fire. By teatime, a passing ship has seen your flag and fire and you are rescued.

## Answers

**1** Top marks if you answered C – you're not only willing and able to learn new things (even if you find them boring), but you can also present your ideas clearly and interestingly. Don't worry if you answered A – you just need to work on your confidence a bit more. If you answered B – Bill Gates will never take you onto his staff unless you change your attitude!

**2** If you answered A, you're a maths mastermind – congratulations! If you answered B, your numeracy skills are the same as most people's. Well done! Keep on working hard. If you answered C, don't give up – Bill Gates would never lose heart and stop trying.

**3** Either B or C is good here, although C is probably better. It's important in business to be able to work well on your own, although you'll often find that you can accomplish more by cooperating as part of a team. (Bill Gates didn't get where he is today by answering A, by the way.)

**4** **A** Bill Gates would never duck out of making an important decision by leaving it up to someone else.

 **B** Bill Gates certainly wouldn't let himself be confused by other people.

 **C** Correct! Bill Gates would have the sense to listen to other people's opinons and then use these to make up his own mind.

**5** **A** The fast-moving computer business is a ruthless, pressurized world. You know

the saying – if you can't stand
the heat . . .

**B** You're certainly creative when
it comes to having ideas and
you're good at solving
problems. But to make it in the
computer business, you need to
be able to
identify what
needs doing
and then
focus your
efforts in the
right direction.
Try not to get so
easily side-tracked.

**C** Bill Gates would be proud of
you. You keep cool under
pressure. You're creative, yet
clear-headed. Your single-
mindedness and determination
gets the right results in double-
quick time.

So if you've got the technical knowledge and the business skills to match, you should be able to cope with working in the hi-tech future, because of course computers are the face of the future. But there are so many different types of computer business to work in and so many different jobs: games writer, graphic designer, sound engineer, webmaster – to mention but a few. So how do you begin working out which one you're going to make your millions at? Reading on should help you make up your mind . . .

# GAMETASTIC!

*I love playing computer games. But a lot of people say that they're a waste of time. Is that true? Do I have to give up playing games and start practising my maths equations instead, if I want to make it in computers?*

You're right, most so-called 'serious computer users' – like teachers, librarians and scientists – look down on games players. Well, they shouldn't. And here's why: if it wasn't for games and games players, many of the most exciting improvements to PCs of the last few years would never have happened. Face it: you don't need a Pentium 3 processor to send a 'happy birthday' email to your Auntie Doris or to type up your Geography project. Come to think of it, you don't even need a colour screen to do those things. But you do to play the latest kick-boxing game, or to drive a Formula One racing car around Monte Carlo (assuming you're not Michael Schumacher or David Coulthard).

The very first computer games were extremely basic compared to what we have now. They looked like the sort of thing any bright geek could knock up in a couple of hours in their bedroom or garage. This isn't surprising, as in many cases that's exactly how they started. Nevertheless, no one had never seen anything like them before and people thought they were incredible (ask your Mum or Dad).

The first computer game sensation was called Pong. No, it wasn't about someone who couldn't stop eating pickled eggs. It was based on ping pong, or table tennis.

The graphics were so simple you wouldn't believe it. There were two rectangles which could be moved from side to side –

those were the bats. And there was a round white ball which was hit from player to player.

*Yawn. How exciting – not!*

I know it sounds incredibly tame today but in the 1970s, when Pong first appeared, everyone thought it was fantastic.

Then came the amazing Space Invaders. These were square-shaped alien blobs who marched down the screen towards you. It was your job to shoot them down with another blob that was supposed to be your alien-zapping gun. But – horror! They shot back at you! It was war to the death! Only you could save the Earth!

Suddenly it was out with Pong and in with Space Invaders! There were stories in the papers about children spending hundreds of pounds on playing the game in amusement arcades, or permanently damaging their zapping fingers from spending all their spare time zapping aliens.

From those humble beginnings came all the games we play now. All the Marios, Sonics, Donkey Kongs, Streets of Rage and Tomb Raiders can be traced back to a few blurry blobs bleeping away in black and white.

In a lot of ways, games-making is the area that has changed most dramatically since the early days of computing. Many people would say that it is the most exciting area of software to work in.

Creating a new computer game is a bit like a game itself. You have to progress from one level through the company to the next. Each level is more difficult and complicated than the last. You have to complete each level before you can go on to the next. If you fail at any of the levels, you can be forced to go right back and start again at the beginning . . .

## PLAYING THE GAME GAME

### Level One: Ideas and Script

Your name is Jo Bloggs and you want to be a computer games writer. First you need an idea . . . No, a **good** idea.

At last – you've got it! An adventure game set in Ancient Egypt called Curse of the Mummy's Tomb. You spend hours on the Internet researching and planning it. You get loads of information and ideas, and you develop your first brainwave. Then you spend months working on it . . . Finally, you present a summary of your ideas, called a concept document, to a group of really important people from the gigantic Mony Corporation. (These bigwigs are thinking about turning your idea into a game for their brand new Paystation 7!) It is the most terrifying experience of your life – like starring in the school play and doing Physics GCSE all rolled into one.

Hooray – the people at Mony, they say yes! They go on to give you a lot of helpful advice about how to write your script. This takes you months and months because it has to be about six times longer than a script for a film. This is because you have to write about six different versions of every major scene, so that players can choose things like which way to go and what to do.

Next, the design team from Mony

turn your script into a flowchart to show all the different paths a player can go down. This diagram is really tricky to draw, but it is vital for the director and art director (who are going to make your game). At last, when the flowchart is finished, you can move on to . . .

## Level Two: Meeting the Team

You go to meet the director, Andy (who is in charge of the whole project), and the art director, Jeff (who decides how everything will look: the sets, the characters, the costumes etc). They don't work directly for Mony, they work for a smaller company, which makes films and animations for a whole range of other companies.

The good news is that you all seem to get on really well. The bad news is that there's still some work to do on the script and the flowchart. Andy and Jeff have been going through it and have spotted some mistakes in the paths: choices that could lead to the wrong places, for instance. Luckily, they're not too serious and are fairly easily corrected.

Andy and Jeff start work on the storyboards. These are like a comic strip of every scene in the game. You think they look great!

Then Jeff the art director goes off to start work on some of the rooms that are going to be the locations for some of the scenes. Like a real action movie, the main characters are going to be played by actors. Andy, the director, tells you the names of the cast. Wow! You've heard of most of them. The actor who is going to play the evil villain used to be one of the leads in a well-known soap – until he got killed off a couple of months ago.

Although the actors are going to be real, most of the sets are going to be drawn on computer. That makes it a lot cheaper than making a feature film, where most of the sets are actually built. But the total budget for your game is still just over $10 million!

You feel like a big shot, even though it's raining and you have to wait half an hour for the bus. Time to go on to . . .

## Level Three: Drawing and Painting

You go to see some of the sets that Jeff, the art director, has been drawing on the computer. Fantastic! They look even better than the scenes you'd imagined when you were writing the script – and they're all in 3D!

Jeff shows you how it's all done. He's got his own team. There's Rick, who draws the backgrounds, and Jean, who draws the characters who are going to be animated, such as all the monsters you've put in your game. Rick works on one computer, drawing the walls, ceilings, floors etc., while Jean works on another. Jean's characters look at first like 3D frames made of wire; she doesn't add any colours or shading to the wireframe models until she's happy with them. When Jeff is happy with Jean's drawings, they put them into Rick's scenes.

Once the sets are finished you can go on to . . .

## Level Four: Filming

You've been invited down to the studios to watch a day's filming. You're so excited you can hardly sleep the night before. That's just as well, because the day's filming starts at 6.30 in the morning! It's too early for you to catch a bus, so Mony send a car to pick you up at 5.15 and drive you to the studio. Glamorous or what?

When you arrive at the studios the shooting is about to begin. But something looks wrong! You were expecting to see those wonderful sets, but the only thing behind the actors is a big blue screen. There are cameras and cables everywhere, and people rushing about. You go and get a cup of tea and sit down to watch. It takes all day to film one scene, because they have to film six different versions for the different choices a player might make.

At the end of the day, you go up to Jeff, the art director. 'What happened to the great sets?' you ask him.

'Come and see the post-production,' he grins.

'What's that?' you ask. But he has already rushed off to the other side of the studio to sort out some props for the next day.

You go out to get the car to go home. On the way back, you realise that you forgot to ask the soap actor for his autograph for your mum.

Not a good day, but now you're ready to go on to . . .

## Level Five: Post-production

You're in the editing suite with Andy, Jeff and two technicians. The editing suite is a small room full of equipment – computers, monitors, speakers, and miles and miles of wires and cables.

'It's quite simple,' explains Andy.

'We've loaded all the digital film of the actors into the computer.'

There is a picture on the screen of the soap actor in his Egyptian costume standing in front of the blue screen. Andy winks at you, clicks his mouse, and everything blue disappears out of the picture. Suddenly the actor is standing in an empty white space.

'Did you notice that we didn't have any blue costumes for filming?' asks Andy. 'If we had done, the actors' bodies would have just disappeared as well! And any actors with blue eyes had to wear different-coloured contact lenses, otherwise their eyeballs would vanish too!'

Andy concentrates for a moment. 'I've got the computer-drawn set ready,' he carries on. 'Just like copy and paste on a word processor, I can put the actor into the set.'

Andy clicks his mouse again and there's the soap actor standing in the middle of a vast Egyptian pyramid!

It takes ages to finish all the scenes; then Andy starts work on adding the soundtrack. This has been written by a composer called Nicola, who specializes in writing music for films, cartoons and TV adverts. The music is carefully cut and edited so that it fits exactly with the action of each scene. Sometimes Andy will use the same piece of music again and again to introduce the character, or when the player comes to the same room, or faces the same hazard.

When you see the final version, you are delighted. It looks and sounds fantastic! So now it's ready for testing, and that is . . .

## Level Six: The Best Job in the World?

A group of people, not much older than you are now, get paid – yes, paid – to play the game to make sure there are no mistakes in it, no fuzzy pictures, no sound effects missing etc. They even check that there are no spelling mistakes in the instructions! Then when all that's done, it's time for . . .

## Level Seven: In the Shops

Curse of the Mummy's Tomb becomes the next games sensation. Mony are so pleased that they give you a contract to work up another ten (at least) games. You are on the way to having a Bill Gates-sized bank account!

**Congratulations!** You have just made it in the world of computer gaming!

# GET RICH WITH GRAPHICS

*I'm a computer graphic designer. Sounds cool, doesn't it? But what the heck does it actually mean?*

Well, graphics really means pictures. So graphic design means sorting out how pictures are going to look on a computer screen (or on a page, if you're working on something you want to print). For instance, how many pictures are you going to have in your document overall? How big or small should they be? What shape should each one have? Which position should each one go in?

But graphic design isn't just to do with pictures. It's just as much to do with typography – what words look like. Your computer will have a whole range of fonts. Some have a fun and

friendly look. Others seem more 'official'.
Others have an instantly recognizable look, such
as medieval handwriting. Graphic designers not
only decide which font is the best for a certain
piece of writing, but also what size the words
should be, how much space there should be
around the words, where the words should go
on the screen (or page) etc.

*But is all this really that important?*

Yes – very. You're much more likely to spend
time at a website or read a
company's advertising
brochure if it looks exciting,
unusual and eye-catching.
Bill Gates would never
have made it big in
computers if his brilliant
Microsoft software had
been packaged and
advertised in a boring,
unimaginative way. Nobody
would have given it a second
look! All this doesn't just make

graphic design a cool and important job, it makes it a cool and well-paid job, too.

*That'll do for me, then!*

Then you need to practise using some graphics. Practice is so important. Anyone can learn to draw on screen using a simple computer paint and draw package, but most people can't be bothered to master more than the boring basics. They try a couple of lines and flat shapes and then get no further. But drawing is like singing or playing an instrument – no matter how good or talented you are, you can only get better if you keep practising. If you asked Bill Gates for his advice on how to make it as a hot-shot computer graphic designer, I'm sure he'd tell you to practise, practise, practise, then practise some more, and keep practising after that, too.

*But I'll have to buy masses of really expensive gear to get a good result!*

Oh no you won't. The basic tools of the graphic designer working on design for a company like Mony are not much different to what you'll have at school, or if you're lucky, at home:

- a computer with drawing, painting and word processing software (basic draw and paint packages come with Windows, if you're using a PC, and Claris, if you're using a Mac)

- a scanner (so you can get photos and pictures that you've drawn freehand on screen to play about with)

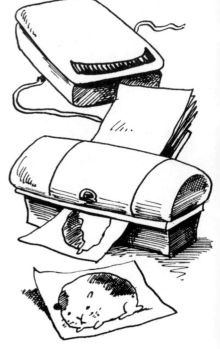

- a printer (so you can see your fantastic results!).

So no excuses, then!

*Well – yes there is, actually. I'm not actually employed by a company like Mony and I haven't got a project to work on.*

Ah, no. Well there is that, I suppose. But there's nothing to stop you making a project up, is there? After all, companies like Mony want people with initiative. What about imagining you're Jo Bloggs and working up a really wicked concept document for Curse of the Mummy's Tomb? How are you going to write and design a summary of the game well enough to make the people at Mony want to give you lots of dosh for it?

Well, there are loads of books, magazines and websites that will tell you how to do really cool things with pictures. You don't need to save up loads of dosh to buy books; a visit to your local library should get you several goodies. You could also try looking in your newsagent at the computer magazines – they often have CDs attached with free programs on them (although you'll have to fork out a couple of quid for the magazine, of course!).

One that's really easy to use is WebArtist; it not only has Clipart, but also photos and even animations. You could also try the website http://www.kidsdomain.com for a good variety of free Clipart and icons. (There are also masses of free games to download and also on-line games to try at this site.)

When it comes to doing zappy things with words, as well as the fonts already installed on your word processor package, you can download free wacky fonts from the Internet, or you could ask your friendly local librarian if the library has CD-ROMs of unusual fonts that you can borrow. Here are a few of my favourites:

This is the perfect font for a review of Robin Hood.

This would be better for the titles for a Vampire movie, but no good for . . .

## ... AN ADVERTISEMENT FOR A COWBOY FILM FROM THE WILD WEST OR ...

... a book about an iron monster made from scrap metal ...

... or a poster for a movie about a **mad, giant, killer mud-creature.**

This font might be good for the cover of a book about polar explorers . . .

... AND THIS ONE MIGHT BE GOOD FOR A REVIEW OF A TV PROGRAMME ABOUT CAVE-PEOPLE.

Get the idea? So now it's over to you. But of course, to make it really big as a computer graphic designer, you need to be able to impress the right people by knowing all the professional tips and shortcuts . . .

## WORK FAST, LOOK GOOD

**If you have a PC running Windows WordPad or Word, instead of the fiddle of going to the File menu, you can:**

■ save a document by just pressing **Control + S** together

■ print by pressing **Control + P** together

■ open a document by pressing **Control + O** together

■ open a new document by pressing **Control + N** together

There are also quick ways to:

■ <u>underline</u> – highlight the bit you want to underline and then press **Control + U** together

■ make something **bold** – highlight the bit you want to make bold and then press **Control + B** together

■ make something *italic* – highlight the bit you want to make italic and then press **Control + I** together

■ cut text – highlight the words you want to cut, then press **Control + X** together

■ move text from one place to another – highlight the words you want to move, then press **Control + C** together. Then move the cursor to where you want to move the text to, and press **Control + V**. Finally, go back and cut the text from its old position.

Best of all, if you make a really stupid mistake (like deleting all your work) – DON'T PANIC! Simply press **Control + Z** together.

It undoes the last thing you did. Phew!

If you have a Mac, the shortcuts in Claris, Appleworks and Word for Macs are exactly the same, but you need to press the Apple key and not Control.

The most important tip of all is to get in the habit of saving your work every 15 or 20 minutes. And don't forget to back up your files on floppy disk at the end of every session on your computer. Even the cutest, friendliest computers can crash from time to time, and when they do, they can

wipe out hours – even days – of work if you haven't saved it safely. Just imagine trying to tell Bill Gates that you'd just wasted a whole week's worth of company time and money because your computer had just wiped out what you were working on – and you didn't have a copy! He wouldn't be impressed now, would he?

So have you finished your concept document for Curse of the Mummy's Tomb yet? You have? Great! Keep up the good work and you'll definitely have what it takes to make it as a computer graphic designer . . .

# WIRED FOR SOUND

As Bill Gates would no doubt tell you, if Mozart was alive today, he'd make sure he was wired

up to some of the hottest computer technology around. Because one of the fastest growing areas of ICT is music. New software and new hardware is being developed at an incredible rate to keep up with the huge number of people who want to compose, record and remix their own music – all on computer. And we're not just talking about the pop industry here. After all, people have to compose, record and remix music for TV programmes, advertisements and feature films too. And what about computer games? The music can often be one of the best bits, adding real atmosphere and excitement.

For Curse of the Mummy's Tomb, Nicola the composer wrote and recorded all the music digitally, using a synthesizer and a computer. She wrote short pieces of music for different places in the game. She also wrote quite short pieces of music – little themes like signature tunes or musical catch-phrases for each character. Each of Nicola's tunes was played into and mixed on a computer, using a system called MIDI.

MIDI stands for Musical Instrument Digital Interface – a posh sounding name that in fact just means 'A Really Great Program That Can Help A Musical Instrument Talk To Your

Computer If You Use The Right Wires And
Stuff'. But as the abbreviation for that is
ARGPTCHAMITTYCIYUTRWAS, people call it
MIDI instead.

*But what about me? Isn't this MIDI equipment
something only the professionals use?*

The chances are that you've already played on
a MIDI-compatible electronic keyboard or
synthesizer in school music lessons, or you might
even own one. Even the simplest keyboard can
produce an amazing variety of sounds. Not only
can it impersonate all the instruments in an
orchestra, from violins to kettle drums, it can
also make sounds like dogs barking, glass
breaking, and spaceships taking off.

*But doesn't the MIDI software itself cost
thousands of pounds?*

No, you can buy the package for under £100.
OK, so you'll have to take on an extra paper-
round and save up your pocket money for
several months, but MIDI's still cheaper than the
latest pair of trainers. And once you've got it,

you'll have an entire orchestra and sound effects studio literally at your fingertips.

*OK, now I'm getting excited. So how does MIDI work, then?*

What MIDI does is to turn all those electronic sounds that your keyboard can make into computer code and back again. That means that the music you play can be not only stored in your computer, but also played back on your keyboard just as you recorded it.

Storing music digitally like this is becoming more and more important to all sorts of musicians who want to make it big. After all, if you live in Ramsbottom-on-Sea, Wales, and you want to play your latest composition to a top film producer in Hollywood, with Midi you don't have to either yodel it down the phone or save up enough money to fly to America in order to thump it out on the piano in person. You can just send it by email as an MP3 file.

Pretty good, huh? But MIDI does much more than that. It actually turns your computer into a complete home studio. Because if you can lay your hands on a CD writer too, you can actually make your own CDs of your own music. So then you're not just a musician and a composer, but a recording company boss as well – and all before you've left school!

*STOP! Hold your horses for one minute! You keep talking about composing. Well, I can't read or write music, so what good is MIDI to someone like me?*

Oh ye of little faith. With a MIDI package, you don't have to be able to read or write music. Sir Paul MacCartney composed both of his orchestral albums using a MIDI program because, despite being one of the most successful (and richest) composers and songwriters who has ever lived, he can't read a note!

That's not to say that with all this fab technology you should just forget about all the old-fashioned stuff. Even with MIDI, being able to read and write music can make life so much easier.

For instance, imagine you've got a brilliant new idea for a song for your band. You could spend hours trying to explain in words, or by waving your arms about, or by making weird woooah woooah or tssssh tssssh noises. Then again, if you and your band can read and write music, by simply scribbling down a few musical notes on paper, you can show them precisely what notes you want them to play, when you want each of them to play, and how loud you want them to be.

Then again, imagine you wake up in the middle of the night with a brilliant idea for a sure-fire number one. If you can read and write music, you can jot it down on a piece of paper and then go back to sleep. If you can't, you'll have to get up, switch on the computer, and switch on your guitar or keyboard. Needless to say, you won't be very popular with your neighbours.

For all these reasons, more and more bands like Blur and The Divine Comedy are getting a formal musical training before they start hitting the charts. And established stars like Elvis Costello who start out not being able to read music are learning after they get famous.

*OK, OK, you've convinced me. I'll make the effort to learn how to read and write music.*

*Later. Perhaps. Right now, all I want to do is get started with making music on my computer. But what am I going to do? I can't possibly wait until I've saved up enough to buy a MIDI package and a synthesizer. It will drive me bananas!*

Fret not! There are magazines like *Computer Music* which include a free CD-ROM or DVD with each issue. These CD-ROMS or DVDs include demonstration versions of music-making programs that you can try out for just the couple of quid that it costs to buy the magazine.

You could also check out websites for free or cheap downloads. There are some great packages you can get off the Internet for next to nothing, or nothing at all.

But best of all, a lot of people don't know that Windows 98 has a sound recording system built in. So as long as you've got a bog-standard PC with Windows 98, there are loads of things you can do . . .

## LEAN MEAN MUSIC MACHINE

**1** Open the **START** menu – that's the button on the left-hand side of the screen with the little Windows symbol.

**2** In the **PROGRAMS** menu, select **ACCESSORIES.**

**3** From the list of accessories, select **ENTERTAINMENT** and click on **SOUND RECORDER.**

A little window will appear with controls that look a bit like a tape-recorder. But what you've got is a basic recording studio. All you need is a microphone (either one built into your computer or, even better, one that can plug into your computer) and you're ready to mix your own tracks.

With this basic system you can:

- record
- add effects to your basic tracks, like echo
  - reverse your track so it will play backwards
  - mix two or more tracks together.

**Congratulations!** Get grooving and you're well on the way to making it in computer music!

# WANNA BE A WEBMASTER?

Can you remember what life was like before we had the Web? When you had to use snailmail (the post) instead of email? When you had to read magazines for up-to-date info instead of accessing websites? When you had to go out and about to make new friends instead of sitting in your bedroom meeting new people on-line?

No, neither can I. That's how important the Web has become to us Earthlings. And the Web is just as important to big businesses (and small businesses too, for that matter), as it is to mere mortals like you and I. Companies can now advertise themselves on-line, sell their goods on-line, recruit staff on-line, do deals with other companies on-line . . . In fact, some companies only 'exist' on-line –they do all their business via their website and they don't run from an office or shop open to the general public at all.

*So who creates these websites, then?*

(I like you – you've got the knack of asking just the right questions at just the right moment, you know.)

Well, that's the job of a webmaster.

*A webmaster? But that sounds like a character out of a sci-fi comic or story . . .*

Yes, yes, I know. The name's a bit over the top, isn't it? Before you get all excited, I should tell you that webmasters don't actually have magical powers. But they do know about all the latest computer technology and they are rather nifty at creating witty and wonderful websites that the likes of you and I want to go to.

Webmasters are also experts at surfing the Net (Internet). Now, the Net can be the ultimate source for finding out information. But, as anyone who's ever spent all Saturday on-line searching for a single homework answer will know, it can also be the biggest waste of time ever! It's the job of a webmaster to know how to find the right information in a fraction of a nanosecond (well, in minutes rather than hours, anyway). They know all the tricks of the trade and can communicate with any computer linked to the Net, anywhere in the world, while looking – not just unflustered - but positively cool.

*So can I make it in computers as a webmaster, then?*

Yes indeedy. As the Net and email become vital to more and more jobs and businesses, webmaster skills are becoming more and more crucial and more and more well paid.

There are two basic things you need to work on:

1 being able to create fab websites

2 being able to surf the Net at the speed of light.

*Isn't it really difficult to build your own website?*

Not any more. It used to be, because web pages have to be written in a special language called HTML (Hypertext Mark-up Language). But now there are lots of programs which do all the hard work for you.

For PCs running Windows there is a program called FrontPage Express, which is included free in some versions of Internet Explorer. Some Apple Macs come with free web page software too – otherwise, there are packages (like WebArtist) that you can buy.

These new, friendly, web-building programs are known as WYSIWYG programs – that stands for *What You See Is What You Get.* And what you get is a window that looks a bit like a word-processor or drawing window. It works by simply pasting in pictures, sounds and words that you've created in your normal text, sound and graphics programs.

Ready to have a go? Right, here's what you do . . .

# ENTER THE WORLD OF THE WEBMASTER

1 Make a rough plan of what words and pictures you want to put on your web page.

2 Open a new folder called something like My Web Page. Then,  using your usual word-processing program, write the text you want on your web page. This could be a piece about yourself, or about your interests (like reviews of your favourite books, games or TV programmes). Save this in your folder.

3 Use your usual graphics package to draw the pictures you want to go on your web page, or get the drawings from Clipart, or

scan in a freehand drawing. Before you save your finished pictures to your new folder, open the **SAVE AS** window in the **FILE** menu. Go to the **SAVE AS TYPE** section and save your drawing as a JPEG file. That'll give you the best results on your web page. (If you want to include photographs, follow exactly the same procedure as for drawings, but if you can, save them as GIF files.)

4   Now open your FrontPage window and simply paste the text and pictures into your new web page from your folder. Don't worry if you don't get it right first time. FrontPage will let you change your mind and alter the position of your words and pics, if you like. All you

have to do is click with your mouse
on an image or block of text and
then drag it to another place on
your page.

5   You don't have to
finish your web
page all at one go.
You can save it and
come back to it
later, just like you
can with any other file. Just save it
into your My Web Page folder. Then
to work on it again, just open
FrontPage (or whatever program
you're using), select **OPEN** from the
**FILE** menu, then **FROM FILE**, and
finally click on **BROWSE** . . . and
there's your page, ready for the
finishing touches.

If you want to have a look at what
your page will look like on the Web,
you can open it using Internet

Explorer. However, you won't be able to work on it in Internet Explorer. To add anything, you'll have to open it through the **FILE** menu in the way I've just told you.

6 So your page is now finished – but it's still in your folder, not on the Web! To get it onto the Web you need to send  your page to your ISP (Internet Service Provider – the people who provide your email and access to the Net). You have to load your page into one of their computers so that it is always available on the Web for anyone who wants to call in. Just phone or email your ISP and they'll tell you what to do. With most ISPs there is no charge for putting your page on the Web.

> (If you're using FrontPage, there is a special Wizard – just like the Wizard that helps you install new software – that can load your page onto the Web for you.)

There you are – that wasn't so difficult was it? And doesn't your page look the business!

Right, you're half way there. Now you need to get to grips with the remaining part of a webmaster's job – surfing the Net. Here are some top tips for getting the most out of the Web . . .

## WICKED WAYS WITH THE WEB

1   If you want to find some information, think about any questions you're going to ask very carefully before you type it into your search engine. This can save you an awful lot of wasted

time. Maybe even write down your question first. For instance, if you want to research information for a concept document for Curse of the Mummy's Tomb, typing in just 'Egypt' will get you a list of more than two million sites! Try sifting through all of those and see how long it takes you to find what you want!

If you use more than one word and put an **AND** or a **+** sign between each word (for instance, Ancient + Egyptian + Pyramids), your search engine will only give you sites that

**Search**

contain all the words. Much more useful.

2   If you're going through a long list of sites, bookmark or add to your favourites list any page that looks interesting or relevant, as soon as you open it. You can always take it off later, but if you move on, you might not be able to remember how to get back to it.

3   Use a specialist engine for kids. If you're looking for homework information, an adult search engine will give you loads of pages filled with advanced mumbo-jumbo that even most adults don't find interesting. A specialist engine will help you find exactly the sort of information you want, at the right kind of level.

You could try:

● **Ask Jeeves for Kids**

http://ajkids.com. Not only a great search engine, it also has message boards where you can leave notes and messages for your mates, and advice about all sorts of things. It also has a special homework search engine.

● **AOL kids only**

http://aol.com/netfind/kids/home. html. Another specialist search engine. Comes with AOL's guarantee of safety (so no Net nasties should pop up to give you nightmares), and you don't have to belong to AOL to use it.

● **Discovery**

http://www.discovery.com. Linked to the Discovery TV channel. Excellent science, nature,

Search

history and geography information – best for teens, as the info can be quite complex.

- **Exam Revision**
  http://www.bbc.co.uk/education/revision. Great site for all exam levels. For Key Stage 3 and revision, look at their Bitesize pages. For Key Stage 2, go to Revise Wise. A big help in bad times!

OK, we're nearly there.

*But I thought you said there were only two main things involved in being a webmaster?*

Yes – but I lied. There's one more thing you need to know about if you want to be a webmaster. One thing that gets Bill Gates shaking in his shoes as he sits in his massive leather chair in his enormous office. One thing that haunts Bill Gates's thoughts as he negotiates million-dollar deals with other top tycoons. One thing that keeps Bill Gates awake at night, tossing and turning feverishly in a cold sweat. And that one thing is . . .

# THE COMPUTER VIRUS!!!

A computer virus is a coded message instructing any computer it infects to do things like erase all files. And viruses can be sent to millions of computers in just a fraction of a second. A really deadly virus could destroy all the computers in a multi-million dollar business in well under a minute. (So now you can see why they're Bill Gates's worst enemy.) If you want to see how even an innocent message can have disastrous results, read *Eclipse of the Century* by Jan Mark.

*So how do webmasters protect themselves from viruses, then?*

Well, there are programs you can buy, like Virex, Norton Anti-Virus, or Dr Solomon, that can detect and destroy computer viruses. But always buy the latest version. New viruses are being invented all the time. If you want to be supersafe, you should never:

- open an attachment to an email, unless you know what the attachment is.

- put a disk into your machine that has been in any machine but your own.

But it's often very difficult to follow these supersafe rules.

*OK, so I can now create web pages that look better than those of the experts, my Net surfing skills are the best in my class, and I'm virus-aware. What now?*

Congratulations! You're now well prepared for the day Bill Gates advertises for staff to work on the Web. Keep up the good work, and you'll make it in computers as a webmaster!

# CLIMBING THE BILL GATES LADDER . . .

Bill Gates started out in computers in the days (about thirty years ago) when a PC came in a kit and you had to build it yourself! So with all the exciting equipment that you can lay your hands on at school and at home nowadays, you've got a great headstart on Bill when it comes to making it in computers.

However, Mr Gates would no doubt say that the very, very best advice for anyone who wants to follow in his footsteps is not just to practise, practise, practise on the machines themselves, but also to stay on at school and get qualifications. As in any desirable industry, there are loads of people after the best jobs. So to stand out as the next hot-shot games writer, graphic designer, sound engineer, webmaster etc., you need to be able to impress possible

employers with all the right official bits of
paper.

### RUNG ONE OF THE BILL GATES LADDER:

Aim to get as many GCSEs as you
can – the more at grades A, B and C,
the better. There's not much point
spending five years at secondary
school (when you'd much rather be
at home mucking
about on your
PC), if you don't
come out with
as many
qualifications as
you can get.

Don't worry if things go wrong – there are second chances. You can retake GCSEs at school or at Sixth Form College or at a College of Further Education. You can also take new subjects at a Sixth Form College or College of Further Education that may not have been offered at your school.

For any job in computers, GCSEs or GNVQs in English, Maths and ICT are a must.

If you want to be a graphic designer, then GCSEs or GNVQs in visual subjects like Art, Graphic Design, Photography, Fashion, or Media Studies are helpful too. If you want to be a sound engineer, then GCSEs or GNVQs in Performing Arts can also be of use.

## RUNG TWO OF THE BILL GATES LADDER:

Get A Levels, A/S Levels, or higher level GNVQs in your best subjects.

Don't be glum about two more years of study. Whether you stay on at school or go to a college, you'll find it's much more fun than studying for GCSEs – you'll be treated much more like a grown-up and you'll be doing only subjects that you really enjoy.

## RUNG THREE OF THE BILL GATES LADDER:

Go on to university, or if you want to be a graphic designer, perhaps to Art School (a well-equipped Art Department will have all the latest computer technology), or if you want to be a sound engineer perhaps a Performing Arts college.

There are hundreds of

£20

courses to choose from, such as: computer science, information technology, computer-aided design, computer animation and film-making, music-making, music technology...etc.

Choose a university or college that has ample facilities for the number of students. It's no good going somewhere that has six G4s if there are 200 students queuing up to use them all the time! Check if they've got good filming and editing suites and recording studios, if that's what interests you.

When you apply, the college may well ask you to show a portfolio of your work (like a coursework folder). As well as the work you've done for school exams, they'll be really interested in the work you do on your own – because that shows your true interests and talents. So get in the habit now of saving the best designs and drawings etc., that you do at home and start building up a cracking portfolio. Bill Gates wouldn't be embarrassed about all the stuff he produced on his home PC, he'd wave it about in front of people, with pride!

## RUNG FOUR OF THE BILL GATES LADDER:

Finally, you get to apply for a job. Today there are more jobs in some areas of computing than others. For instance, at the moment there are fewer jobs for computer animators than for graphic designers. This is because not everything needs moving images, but everything printed (such as books, magazines, plastic carrier bags from the supermarket etc.) has to be designed.

However, by the time you leave college, there will be new jobs that don't exist now. Fifteen years ago there was no such job as a webmaster. Now there are lots of opportunities for web designers. In another few years, there may be fewer of these jobs as the software gets easier and easier for an amateur to use. But there may be some new job that will be really popular then that hasn't even been dreamed of yet. That's the excitement of working with computers . . .

So, as I'm sure Bill Gates would want to wish you, good luck!

# GLOSSARY

**Bold**     A heavier, blacker version of a font

**Circuit**    The pathway that an electric current takes as it flows along is called a circuit. Information in the form of tiny electrical signals is passed around circuits and microchips in a computer.

**Clipart**    A type of artwork which may be provided on your computer or on disk. These pictures can be added to documents you create on your computer.

**Cursor**    An on-screen tool you use to select or move objects or to enter text. You control the movement of the cursor by moving the mouse. The cursor is shown as a pointer arrow or I-beam on screen.

**Email**     Electronic mail is the term used for typing a document into one computer and delivering it to another. Email enables you to transmit messages anywhere in the world in seconds.

**Flow chart**   A diagram which shows the stages of a process e.g. the steps in a computer program

**Font**     Typeface

**Hardware**   Refers to the physical parts of a computer system such as the monitor and keyboard.

**ICT**      Information Computer Technology

**Italic**     A sloping type used when you want to emphasise part of the text

**Internet, the**  The Internet is a large system linking millions of computers around the world

**IT**            Information Technology

**Microchip**    A very thin slice or 'chip' of silicon with thousands or millions of tiny electronic parts. Each chip does a certain job like hold memory for a computer or carry out the computer's main processing.

**On-line**      On-line means that your computer is directly connected to another computer or group of computers.

**Search engine** A search engine allows you to search the World Wide Web for specific data and to find your way through the information contained on the Internet

**Silicon**      A non-metallic element. Microchips are made from small pieces of silicon

**Software**     This term refers to computer programs and accessories such as disks.

**Spreadsheet**  Information presented in rows and columns of cells. You can use spreadsheets to list and analyse data

**Synthesizer**  A computerised instrument for making sounds

**Wap phone**    A mobile phone with the capacity to access the Internet

**Web, the**     A system that enables people connected to the Internet to view text, graphics, sounds and movies.

**Website**      The basic document available for viewing information on the Internet

**Word processing** Using a computer to electronically type, arrange and store text.